Old Balmedie and Belhelv

Rosie Nicol

Salmon fishers at Menie Fishing Station.

© Rosie Nicol, 2023
First published in the United Kingdom, 2023,
by Stenlake Publishing Ltd.
54-58 Mill Square,
Catrine, KA5 6RD
www.stenlake.co.uk
ISBN 978-1-84033-951-2

The publishers regret that they cannot supply
copies of any pictures featured in this book.

Printed by
Blissetts, Unit E1-E8 Shield Drive,
West Cross Ind Pk, Brentford, TW8 9EX

Rosie Nicol   April 2023

ACKNOWLEDGEMENTS

This book has been several years in the making. Over that time I have learned a lot from many people in Belhelvie parish and beyond. Special thanks go to my friends and advisers Pat Newman and Janet Jones. My thanks also go to:

Gordon Raffan, Margaret Murison, Pat Leslie, David Leslie, Sheila Lamb, Atholl Lipp Jnr., Jess Petrie, Penny Gravill, Mary Cane, Ian Thomson, Rita Mands, Bill Leith, Bill Reid, Jonathan Holt, Julie Gordon, Mark Mitchell, Shelley Carr, Val Fowlie, Sandy and Vi May, Cecil Craig, Malcolm Forbes, Lee Fowlie, Jenny Nicol, Mike Mitchell, Gordon Pirie and The Cock and Bull, as well as John Easton, for photographs donated by Jim Forbes. I have not been able to use all their information in this book, but I hope to create a permanent archive in Balmedie so that their knowledge of our local history will not be lost for present and future generations.

James Morrison Photographic Collection

Several of the photographs in this book come from the James Morrison Photographic Collection, courtesy of the Buchan Heritage Society who provided the information below.

James Morrison was born in 1865 to farmer William Morrison and his wife Jane Murray at Newseat of Schivas in the parish of Tarves. He was the eldest of five children. The family moved to a fifty acre farm, Stoneyards in the parish of Belhelvie, around 1870 where later James worked alongside his father. James married Helen Riddell in 1911 at the age of forty six and had three of a family. His son, also James, became a policeman in London and his two daughters Mary and Rosa did not marry and continued to stay in the family home at Menie.

He was a very sociable man with an interest in the traditions and played the pipes and the fiddle. He was a very distinguished member of the coast guard service, serving for fifty years. After coming off the farm he started up as cycle agent at his home at Menie. He died there in 1952 and is buried in Belhelvie Churchyard.

James is mostly remembered for his photographs of Aberdeenshire and is believed to have taken up photography as a hobby in the 1880s achieving a very high degree of skill. His photographic plates were discovered in 1985 in an old blocked up cupboard in the farmhouse at Stoneyards during renovations.

The plates were later passed to the Buchan Heritage Society, giving them sole ownership and copyright, with the support and approval of James Morrison's two daughters. Some work was carried out on the collection at that time by the late Eric Ellington with financial support from BP.

The collection consists of over six hundred and fifty glass plate negatives, all of which have now been digitised. They mostly depict rural life in an area north of Aberdeen from 1890 to 1925 looking at portraits of families and farm workers, the farms and crofts of that time and particularly the horses and the dedicated men who worked the land. The collection covers a wide and diverse view of life; the prints include people from all levels of society, a glimpse of the work and daily toil of people in the late 19th and early 20th centuries and particularly the First World War period. They also show the great pride and relationship of men and horse.

Introduction

Belhelvie is a country parish, directly to the north of Aberdeen, bounded by sea, sand dunes and beaches to the east and rural parishes to the west. Prior to the discovery of oil in the North Sea it was a parish of farming, fishing, clay workings, quarrying and all the country trades needed for every day life.

This book gives a glimpse of a Scottish rural parish over 150 years, from the reign of Queen Victoria to that of her great- great- great grandson King Charles. According to census information, the population of 1,692 in 1851 had risen to 5,082 by 2011. In Queen Victoria's days only a few people owned houses and most rented from wealthy landowners. The 1870 valuation roll shows that most of the properties in the parish of Belhelvie were owned by just 14 wealthy individuals, plus one estate owned by the Society of Advocates, who had many tenants in cottages, farms and crofts. There are still some rented properties in the parish, but the majority of people now own their own homes.

During the last 30 years of the 19th century, there was considerable development in the parish with many more houses being built by the landlords. Some photographs available to me showed a few of these properties, so this seemed an interesting period to look at first. Coincidentally, a friend found a copy of the 1870 valuation roll for this area at a sale, so that encouraged my starting point of 1870. Just 100 years later in the 1970s, there was another, much larger expansion of the parish when the oil industry boomed in Aberdeen and the North Sea.

In 1870 the parish was divided into large estates: Ardo, Balmedie, Craigie, Belhelvie Lodge, Blairton, Wester Hatton, Menie, Millden, Muirton, Rannieston (part), Tilliery, Gateside, Whitecairns, Potterton and Orrock.

Unlike today, there were no settlements of more than a few houses as people lived in individual properties on these estates, paying rents for their farms, crofts, shops, workshops and cottages to the landowners. These tenants mostly relied on the estate owners for their work and pay. In 1930s the estates were beginning to be split up and people were buying their own houses.

Today the parish consists of five settlements plus many smaller developments and individual properties. The five are Balmedie, Belhelvie, Blackdog, Potterton and Whitecairns. With the expansion of the oil industry these villages have grown, but Belhelvie parish is still a place where agriculture and the sea are hugely important in creating a sense of place.

It's 1945 and the Second World War has ended in Europe. Horses and carts, owned and driven by Sim Brothers from Keir Farm, carry happy children from Balmedie village along the road to Menie House for a picnic and celebrations.

Balmedie House seen here from the north-west showing the clock tower dates from 1878 when the original single storey building was substantially extended by William Harry Lumsden. In 1879, it was reported that the house could be clearly seen from the Ellon Road, but the trees have grown into mature woodland obscuring it from view. William Harry was the son of William James Lumsden who made a fortune in Bombay as a magistrate and then judge with the Honourable East India Company. William Harry Lumsden married Elizabeth Renny Tailyour in Montrose in 1877. They went on to have seven children. To the outside world a privileged family, they had more than their fair share of tragedy and sadness. William Harry died in 1900 of a liver tumour aged just 47 years, leaving his wife with an estate to run and a family of six to care for. A seventh child had died as a baby in 1888. Three sons, Harry Tailyour Lumsden, Charles Ramsay Lumsden and Bertie Noel Lumsden died during the First World War. Elizabeth Lumsden died in 1917, aged just 64 years and the estate passed into the hands of her son, Ernest Francis Lumsden. Balmedie Estate remained the property of the Lumsden family until Ernest's death in 1932 when it was sold to Castiglione, Erskine & Co in London, who then sold off parts of the estate. Existing tenants of farms, crofts, cottages and commercial concerns were given the chance to buy their buildings, the Department of Agriculture bought some properties to include in their Small Holdings Scheme, and the Church of Scotland bought Balmedie House to convert to an eventide home.

The original Balmedie House from the 1860s was described as a 'plain but substantial mansion house' of 19 rooms. It was built of granite from Udny, and dressed with yellow sandstone from Elgin. Once extended by William Harry Lumsden, it contained 44 rooms. It is a Category C listed building sitting in 26 acres of grounds. The roof slates above the turret are in a fishtail pattern to accommodate the conical shape whilst the remainder of the roof is traditional. The crow or corbie stepped gables are reminiscent of Jacobean Scottish architecture. In 1870 the estate included six farms, cottages, crofts, a smithy and salmon fishings. The estate expanded during William Harry's ownership with the building of houses, police station and shops in Balmedie village. Since 1935 the house has been a residential and care home for up to 24 older people. The original house has been extended. Properties around the house, including the former butler's cottage, and the stable block on the way to the beach, have been converted into private dwellings.

DINING ROOM, BALMEDIE EVENTIDE HOME

The dining room of Balmedie House with tables laid for dinner, immaculate white tablecloths and bentwood chairs, typical of the 1930s when the photograph was taken. This was an elegant dining room with a panelled ceiling to imitate coffered ceilings of a bygone age. The walls have heavily decorated wainscoting with similar heavy moulding to the doors and the fireplace. The over-mantle is of Victorian design with inserted mirrors and detailed decorative features. When the house was a private dwelling, the mirrors allowed the servants to discreetly observe whether diners had finished eating and plates could be cleared away. There is a dresser against the wall. As its proportions emulate the panelling it would seem to have been designed specifically for this room.

BEDROOM, BALMEDIE EVENTIDE HOME

When Balmedie House was converted into an eventide home in 1930s, the residents slept in dormitories separated by curtains to afford a little privacy. This layout was common for the time and resembled a hospital ward. Each resident had a bed, a cupboard, a chair and a towel! Note that there was only a centre light so no late night reading. Thankfully, residents now have their own rooms.

This photograph of a snowy day in Balmedie Village was sent as a postcard in 1910. The telegraph poles were erected in 1885 when the village had its first telegraph connection. A newspaper article of 25th July 1885 states:- *"The postal centre hitherto known as Eggie, in the parish of Belhelvie, will be known by that name no more. At any rate, from this time the postmark of that centre will be '**Balmedie**' and to the parishioners and others the place in future will be known as '**Balmedie Village**" instead of 'Eggie.' The change of name has been inaugurated by a change of still more importance to the parishioners of Belhelvie, inasmuch as the village has been dignified by direct connection with the postal telegraphs, a telegraph office having been opened at Balmedie Village."* On the left is the police house and station, built and owned by the Lumsden family of Balmedie House but rented to Aberdeen County Council. Beyond are houses built by Harry Lumsden to house estate workers, farmers and fishermen and to provide a general store for the village. On the right is Mr Forbes joiner's workshop. Today, the police house has gone, replaced by flats and one commercial property. Some of the houses remain, including the two in the distance which became part of the 36 Holdings, created when Balmedie Estate was sold in 1930s. Some of the elm trees on the right were felled to allow the construction of Balmedie Garage. One large elm still stands. Out of sight to the right is the Smithy, the oldest surviving house in Balmedie village.

Taken in the 1930s or 1940s, Balmedie Garage on the right has Esso petrol and oil for sale. This building was badly damaged by fire in October 1979 and rebuilt on a slightly different site. The police house is on the left. Some locals remember PC Jamieson and his musical family in 1950s. Mrs Jamieson trained a choir and organised concerts in the area. Belhelvie Church is in the distance to the far left. Since the snowy picture, the road has been built up and resurfaced to accommodate motor vehicles.

These are some of the houses built by William Harry Lumsden, who owned Balmedie Estate in Victorian times. This postcard view was posted in 1905 from Overhill, Balmedie to Blairythan, Foveran and shows the Balmedie Shop and Post Office, with the names of the tenants Alexander and Jessie Hutchison over the door. The Hutchisons delivered goods by wheelbarrow. The houses were close to the road at the front, but had communal land at the back for drying clothes and children's play. In 1901 one of these houses was occupied by Mr Rae, a carpenter and also an Inspector of the Poor on behalf of the local Parochial Board. As such, he was responsible for reviewing applications for relief under the Poor Law (Scotland) Act 1845 and for taking to court those who failed to provide for their families thus making them a financial burden on the Parish. People who applied for and were granted poor relief were called paupers and their names were entered onto a roll kept by the Parochial Board. Poor relief could be a small amount of money or an admission to the dreaded Poor House or Workhouse where conditions were harsh. There does not appear to have been a Poor House in the parish but there is evidence of Belhelvie paupers in Old Machar Union Workhouse in Aberdeen.

Most of the properties here were built by William Harry Lumsden. The building marked with a cross has been home to a draper and clothier, a telephone exchange, a hairdresser and currently as a therapy clinic and a fish and chip shop. The gable in the centre of the picture was at one time the Whitehorse Inn, owned by the Lumsden family. Beyond it is Mr Forbes the joiner's workshop with the smithy next door. When the 1920 valuation roll was compiled, Balmedie village was made up of twelve dwelling houses, a couple of shops, a police house, smithy and joiner's workshop. Tenants of those houses included a farmer, a salmon fisherman, a postman, a tailor and a road-man. The field in the foreground complete with hay stook was part of a steading owned by Mr Pegler who later built a shop to replace Mr Hutchison's shop. The chimneys of his steading house can just be seen over the roof of the barn on the right. The tailor was Mr Ferguson, whose daughter Alice ran the draper's shop and the telephone exchange which was housed at the back of their shop. The old Whitehorse Inn became two houses, one of which was the home of Mr Urquhart who worked as a tailor for Mr Ferguson, then became a tailor for Aberdeen Police, making uniforms.

A different view of the shops, slightly earlier I think as no sign yet of telephone wires. The building has been extended to the left and used over the past forty years as a general shop, a hairdresser and a therapy clinic.

Balmedie Shop in 1974. This building combining village shop, post office and savings bank was built by George Pegler at right angles to his steading house which contained four rooms, kitchen and bathroom. The Pegler family were in Portsmouth in the early 1800s and had settled in the North East by 1841, becoming fruit merchants in Aberdeen. An article in *Aberdeen Press and Journal* in 1936 mentions that Mr and Mrs Pegler had a tea room here which *"seems to be enjoying a fair patronage from residents in the district and an occasional wayfaring visitor."* The shop was typical of its type selling essentials to the local population. The advertising indicates cigarettes and newspapers were sold as well as the locally famous Holburn Ices. After many years of service the shop is now derelict, empty and roofless, awaiting development.

An aerial view from the east, taken in 1978, of Balmedie village. In the foreground is the roof of the then new Balmedie Primary School, Forsyth Road and Drive, parts of Old Mill Crescent and Burnside Way. There are houses on North Beach Road. Whitehorse Terrace looks complete with Whitehorse Inn beyond, towards the top of the photo. The surrounding farmland would soon be developed for housing.

Still growing, and more to come... Balmedie from the west (the primary school is in the top left corner) taken in 1985. Old Mill Crescent is now a complete horseshoe shape, houses have been built on land which was formerly part of Eigie Farm. Eigie House sheltered housing complex is visible as is the roof of Balmedie Leisure Centre, built on the site of the demolished Eigie Farmhouse.

Keir Farmhouse probably around 1900 when ladies' large hats were in vogue! In the 1870 Valuation Roll, William Emslie was the tenant and the farm was described as having a good substantial farm steading on the Estate of Balmedie. At some time after this photograph was taken, there was a serious fire that destroyed a large part of this house. It was rebuilt on the same site in a more modest form and is a family home today. Margaret Murison lived at the cottar house at Keir Farm as a small child during the Second World War and remembers when, in broad daylight when they were having tea and her mum was taking in the washing, bombers flew over Balmedie House and dropped an incendiary on the farm which set fire to stored straw. The villagers brought water from Eigie Burn and put the fire out, and all was well!

In 1933 the Government embarked on a land settlement scheme, where houses with an area of land would be rented to tenants with the aim of encouraging people to settle in the countryside. The experiment coincided with the sale of Balmedie and Blairton Estates in 1932 following the death of Ernest Lumsden. Eggie Farm and Keir Farm were sold to the Department of Agriculture for Scotland who in 1935 created 36 smallholdings on the land, each with house and land from four to 20 acres. Some smallholdings had to be built while other holdings incorporated existing estate houses. The new-build houses were larger than traditional croft houses, usually with four rooms and a kitchen. Rents were higher than older crofts, but comparable to a similar house in Aberdeen which would not have the land or bathrooms. The aim was to encourage self sufficiency by bringing people back to working the land. Land was used for poultry farming, pig keeping, and fruit and vegetable growing. One settler established a cosy little refreshment room.

To the west of Balmedie lies Belhelvie village, much of which also owed its existence to the Lumsden family. Taken from the south-east, this photograph shows the ivy-clad façade of Belhelvie Lodge which was built in 1783 by Harry Lumsden, an advocate who was the father of William James Lumsden who lived at Balmedie House. The house has a hipped or piend slated roof and the walls are granite. The east wing was added around 1800 with harled granite walls, the granite being evident in quoins or corner stones. A conservatory was added at around this time.

In 1832 the estate passed into the hands of Harry's third son, Colonel Thomas Lumsden CB and his wife Hay Burnett with whom he had eleven children. After Sir Thomas died, ownership of the estate passed to his son, Harry Burnett Lumsden, and his wife Fanny Myers. Harry was born on board

the ship *Rose* in the Bay of Bengal. He was often known as Lumsden of the Guides because of his role in the Indian Army. Speaking near perfect Punjabi, he was asked to form a Corps of Guides at Peshawar in 1846 as a highly mobile force of cavalry and infantry companies. In 1848, Harry and his fellow officer William Hodson decided to use camouflage uniforms for the Guides and chose khaki (from the Urdu word for dust coloured). In 1868, British troops adopted the colouring for campaign dress and the colour has been used by armies across the world ever since. On returning to Belhelvie, Sir Harry continued his hobby of hawking which he had first taken up in the Hindu Kush. He also became an award winning wood carver and an accomplished photographer.

Harry died in 1896. Fanny lived until 1919. As well as Harry, two other sons of Thomas and Hay followed their father into the Indian Army and served with distinction. William was killed in action at the age of 26 and Peter (Sir Peter Stark Lumsden) rose to the rank of General. Thomas and Hay's other three sons emigrated to Canada. Of their five daughters, Helen married Rev James Johnstone of Potterton United Free Church, Katherine married John Paton of Grandhome, Mary Ann married Captain George Cleghorn of the Scots Greys and Edith married Francis George Sherlock, an army captain. Clementina Jane did not marry. Because of the terms of the entail on the estate, it eventually passed to Isabella Hay Lumsden who died without heirs. The estate was then sold out of the family.

Taken from the south-east this photograph shows the village of Belhelvie before the quarry was opened and its associated worker's housing built. In addition to Belhelvie Lodge mansion house, the Lumsden family also owned Belhelvie Lodge Estate. This small village housed two tailors, two shoemakers, a gardener and two wrights (probably blacksmiths or joiners). Over the following decades, these trades were supplemented by a grocer, a midwife, a watchmaker and a milliner. The village was largely self-sufficient in the 19th century. In 1919, Aberdeenshire County Council opened Balmedie Quarry on land owned by Captain Ernest Lumsden of Balmedie House. To house the quarrymen and their families, the Council built two terraces of twelve single storey dwellings in blocks of two. These were Scott Terrace and Park Terrace which formed the first expansion of the village. Recently housing has been built to the east of the old village. The bowling green is on ground gifted by a local landowner to ex-servicemen returning from the First World War. Between 1918 and 1924 the area was used for the game of quoits. Eventually bowls took over and in 1924 the Belhelvie Bowling Club was formed.

Balmedie Quarry on the outskirts of Belhelvie was first excavated in 1919 on land owned by Lumsden of Balmedie on the adjacent farms of Rocks of Balmedie and Parks of Balmedie. In 1920, the Valuation Roll states that Captain Ernest Francis Lumsden of Balmedie owned the quarry which was leased to Aberdeen County Council. In 1930 Captain Lumsden was also the proprietor of Shiels Quarry near Orrock. He died in 1932 at the age of 49 and his estate was broken up and sold. By the 1935 Valuation Roll, Shiels was noted to be 'unwrought' and owned by Castiglione, Erskine and Co. and Balmedie Quarry was owned by Aberdeen County Council, as was part of the farm of Park of Balmedie. This quarry, still in operation, is owned by Aberdeenshire Council. Unlike many quarries in Aberdeenshire, the stone is gabbro and not granite. Like granite gabbro is a coarse grained igneous rock, but its mineral composition is similar to basalt. It is a dark granular rock and, in the case of Balmedie Quarry, is used for road stone. In the top picture a deck of drum screens used to grade the rock by size as it passes down through various screens. A large number of men were employed in the quarry. The *Aberdeen Journal* of 13th October 1925 reported that "*the Aberdeen District Committee approved a report by the Roads Sub-Committee recommending the adoption of a scheme for the erection of six blocks of cottages to accommodate twelve families at a total estimated cost of £4902*". That price equates to around £300,000 today! The scheme went ahead, and those cottages are still there, nearly 100 years old.

The drum screens of Belhelvie Quarry are in the background in this photograph of a Foden steam wagon used for transporting quarried materials to the point of use. The Foden Company was started by Edwin Foden in the 1870s and originally produced large industrial engines, stationary steam engines and agricultural engines. Steam engines were not used to power lorries on the road until after 1896 when restrictions were lifted and vehicles under three tons were allowed to travel at up to 12mph with the need for a man to walk ahead carrying a red flag. Just after the turn of the 20th century, Foden developed a very successful steam lorry and these were produced until 1935 when diesel became the fuel of choice.

Muirton House of Muirton, sometimes known as Muirtown or Meadowbank, was part of the extensive Panmure Estate until it was forfeit to the Crown in 1715. The name Muirton probably stems from the time when rough moorland was drained and taken into cultivation. In 1782 the estate was sold to James Reid, a merchant in Banffshire. On his death, the estate passed to his nephew, Peter Reid, who married Ann Lumsden of Belhelvie. They had a son, James Reid, who inherited the estate which consisted of the mansion house along with several farms and crofts. James was an eminent physician who became 'physician in ordinary', resident physician, to three successive monarchs – Queen Victoria, King Edward VII and George V. James was knighted in 1895 and made a baronet in 1897 in recognition of his service to Queen Victoria. Sir James provided emotional and palliative care to the Queen at the end of her life. In 1899 Sir James married the Honourable Susan Baring, of the Baring banking family, who had been maid of honour to Queen Victoria. The property was sold in 1877 to Alexander Sim and later to the Ligertwood family. The house is now surrounded by trees but the open fields between the Potterton Road and the house are largely unchanged with the area untouched by development. In springtime, the grounds of the house are covered in snowdrops.

Whitecairns is a small settlement which grew up along the road from Aberdeen to Tarves, towards the northern boundary of Belhelvie Parish. This house, on the main road in Whitecairns, has been extended and has a garage attached. Before the First World War Mr and Mrs Cobban sold refreshments, tea, coffee, tobacco and cigarettes here. Mr Cobban was also a shoemaker and cycle agent, operating from a wooden workshop nearby. The front elevation of the house is a fine example of Aberdeen Bond. Each course of granite ashlar blocks is separated by three small, square-section stones set one above another. The chimney pots are late Victorian or early Edwardian so date the house to that era.

The valuation roll of 1870 shows Whitecairns Estate as owned by Sir Charles Forbes of Newe and comprising three farms, four crofts, an inn and a schoolhouse. The Forbes family were known for their charitable works, including a donation of £10,000 for the building of Cornhill Hospital in Aberdeen and further payments for ongoing maintenance of the building.

MIDDLEMUIR   *Courtesy of Buchan Heritage Society*

In 1879 Middlemuir Farm was part of Ardo Estate, the neighbouring estate to Whitecairns, and was owned by Peter Harvey then his children William, James and Susan Harvey. According to the valuation roll of 1870, Ardo belonged to the trustees of the late Peter Harvey. Apart from the mansion house of Ardo and the mansion house of Middlemuir, the estate consisted of the Home Farm of Middlemuir with gardens and woodlands, the Home Farm of Ardo, six crofts and seven farms. William, James and Susan were deaf from birth (census of 1871). Their uncle, William Harvey supported a Deaf and Dumb Institution in Aberdeen, and the Magdalen penitentiaries which provided accommodation and support for vulnerable women.

King Robert the Bruce granted the lands of Menie and Blairtown to John de Boneville in the 14th century and after several owners, the land reverted to the Crown. John Seton of Auquhorties acquired the land in 1610 from King James VI. The house is marked on Blaeu's map of 1654. There were several owners in the 17th century including William Forbes (Danzig Willie), a prosperous merchant, and George Gordon of Gight (forefather of Lord Byron). In the late 1700s the estate was purchased by Robert Turner of the Turner Hall, Ellon. His son, George Turner, commissioned John Smith to design the house as seen above around 1835. Like Danzig Willie, the Turners had been successful merchants trading with Danzig, but George Turner was a military man and became a general. His only son died in infancy so his estate devolved to his daughters, Catherine, Helen and Robina whose names appear on the valuation roll of 1870. The present house is a Category B listed building, designed by Aberdeen architect John Smith around 1835 for Sir George to replace an earlier house which stood on the site. It is a handsome building with dormer-heads, a circular tower and an impressive porch in the Tudor style. It was the mansion house of Menie Estate which in 1870 included twelve farms, crofts, salmon fishings, a smithy, a porter's lodge, and four Coast Guard houses at Leyton: Admiralty Buildings, owned by the Admiralty. General Sir George Turner served with distinction in the Royal Artillery at the Battle of Cape Town, which resulted in the establishment of British rule in South Africa, and in the Peninsular War in Europe. Menie House is today owned by Donald Trump who has renamed it McLeod House in honour of his mother.

Sir George Turner owned Menie School and paid the teacher's salary. After his death his daughters Catherine and Robina were similarly involved with the school. An annual picnic and games was held in the grounds of Menie House for the children, who are shown here passing the front door of the house in a procession led by piper James Morrison. Robina Turner was also a patron of the Young Woman's Association, Belhelvie Branch.

Belhelvie Old Church was dedicated to St Columba and also known as Pettens Church, after the nearby farm. The churchyard is Category C listed and the church is Category B listed. This church was built in 1762 and stands on the site of a pre-Reformation original. It is now mostly in ruins, with just the west gable surviving. Its birdcage bell-cote survives, dated 1762 T.R. (Thomas Ragg, who was minister 1745-1766). The bell, dated 1633, was stolen in 1966! The church was built from roughly-coursed granite rubble, with slightly better quality granite blocks in the surviving south section of the south wall. The west gable has a rectangular door at ground level with a rectangular window above at gallery level.

It was replaced by the present Belhelvie Church of Scotland Parish Church, at one time called Belhelvie North Church, which was built between 1876 and 1878. There were also churches in other parts of the parish. In 1843, Thomas Clapperton, a druggist, donated land to the parish to build Belhelvie Free Church and School in Potterton. The Shiels United Presbyterian Church, built in 1791, amalgamated with Belhelvie Free Church in 1905 and formed the Belhelvie and Shiels Free Church which closed in 1908. The congregation then worshipped in Potterton, at Belhelvie South Church. In 1953 Belhelvie South Church amalgamated with Belhelvie North Church, and together they became Belhelvie Parish Church. The Potterton church building was sold and became a private house.

The graveyard is situated in the countryside to the north of Balmedie in an imposing setting near the sea. It tells a story of an agricultural and fishing parish, where people worked hard in difficult conditions on land and sea. Buried next to each other are landowners and their tenants, farmers, fishermen and sailors, many children who died young and young men who were killed in wars. Also buried here are the public servants; the ministers, teachers, coastguards and inspectors of the poor and the tradesmen; blacksmiths, masons, millers, wrights, and tailors.

There are several notable residents buried in the churchyard including the Rev. Alexander John Forsyth (1769-1843) who is mentioned later in the book. This photo shows the graves of the Lumsden family of Balmedie and Belhelvie. Also buried here are General Sir George Turner of Menie House, and Rev William Thomson (1815 – 1887) who was 44 years minister of the parish.

(The Kirkyard of Belhelvie has been indexed by the North-East Scotland Family History Society, and is available online and in booklet form)

In the graveyard are, unusually, two morthouses, where bodies were temporarily stored before a formal funeral took place. These buildings date back to the time when body snatchers or resurrectionists illegally exhumed dead bodies that were then sold for dissection as part of human anatomy training at universities. In Belhelvie Churchyard one morthouse is a small turf-covered and vaulted structure, set mostly below ground, with steps down to the entrance. The other is a larger, stone 1835 building in the corner of the graveyard. It is rectangular and has a wooden door. After its original purpose ceased it was used for temporary reception of bodies of seamen drowned on the neighbouring coast. It is now a store.

Near to the churchyard is the former parish manse built by Robert Smith, mason, in 1768-69, now a private house.

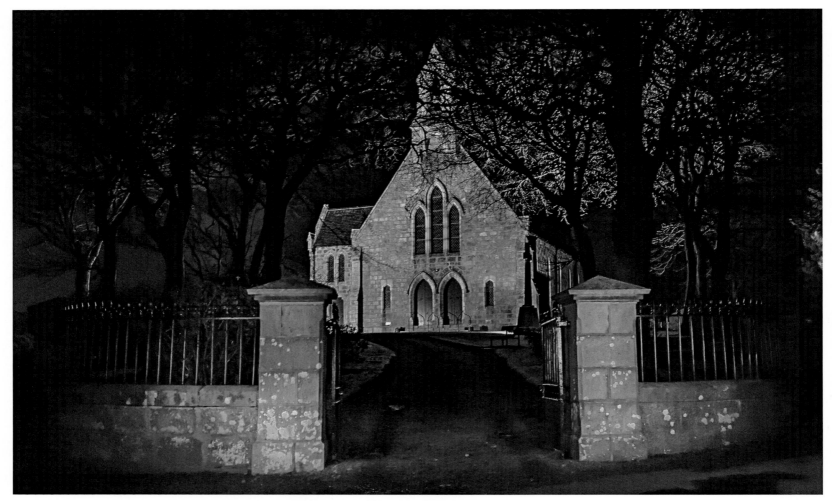

In 1876 plans were set in motion to replace the 1762 Belhelvie Old Church with a new one. The architect was R William Smith, and the cost of building the church was £2,622. The land was donated to the parish by its owner, William Harry Lumsden of Balmedie House. The new church opened as Belhelvie North Church in 1878. In 1953 it was united with the Belhelvie South Church in Potterton to become the Parish Church. Over its first 100 years, until the centenary in 1978, there were only four ministers, the Reverends Thomson, Sorley, Ewen and Forsyth.

Alexander John Forsyth was born at Belhelvie Manse on December 28th 1768 and baptised on New Year's Day 1769. He was the son of Rev John Forsyth of Belhelvie, whom in 1791 he succeeded as minister of Belhelvie Old Kirk. He is mostly remembered for his knowledge of firearms but he was a man of many interests who served his community well.

He was educated at King's College, Aberdeen graduating MA in 1786 and later awarded LLD in 1834 *"as a mark of esteem for his private character and for his attainments in science"*.

As well as his parish duties, Rev Forsyth had a blacksmith's smiddy in the grounds of the manse and earned the nickname of Hammer and Tongs.

He appears to have been a powerful preacher as he sometimes had as many as 700 people attending Sunday service. As the church was designed to hold 519 parishioners, it seems that they were prepared to endure considerable discomfort to hear him!

Rev Forsyth began a savings bank for the parish. The idea behind the Savings Bank Movement was to give poorer people a place to keep their money and to encourage saving. In Scotland, the bank was usually run by the incumbent of the Parish Church. In Belhelvie, Rev Forsyth reported in 1840 that the local savings bank had stock amounting to £600. By one method of calculation – the price of commodities, this equates to £51,000 at present day buying power.

He was also interested in public health. Vaccination to provide protection against smallpox had been carried out by Edward Jenner in Gloucestershire since 1796 and was being widely used throughout Scotland in the early part of the 19th Century. Rev Forsyth brought vaccinations to Belhelvie parish, carrying out the procedure himself!

In 1840, he wrote the Belhelvie section of the *New Statistical Account* of Scotland which was published in 1845, two years after his death.

A keen wildfowl hunter, he was dissatisfied with the firing mechanism of the flintlock shotgun and set about inventing a better system. In 1807, he had perfected his mechanism and took out a patent to protect it from imitation. Although designed for fowling guns, the British Army were interested enough to provide him with facilities to develop his idea in the Royal Armouries in London. However, this was withdrawn when a new Master-General of Ordnance was appointed. It is said that Emperor Napoleon was sufficiently interested in the invention to offer Rev. Forsyth a large sum of money for his invention which he declined. Later, the British Government decided to award him a small pension but the first instalment arrived on the day he died so he did not get any benefit from it. Eventually, his invention was further improved to provide the percussion cap firing system. He and his invention are remembered in plaques at the Tower of London and at King's College, Aberdeen University.

More can be read about his invention in *The Reverend Alexander John Forsyth and His Invention of the Percussion Lock* by Sir Alexander John Reid.

Alexander John Forsyth died on 11th June 1843 of heart disease at the age of 75 and is buried alongside his father in Old Belhelvie Kirkyard. He is remembered in 1929 by a memorial in the Tower of London, a replica of which was erected in 1931 on the Cromwell Tower, where he conducted experiments, at King's College in Aberdeen.

The Belhelvie War Memorial in Belhelvie Church of Scotland churchyard is a grey granite Celtic cross with central boss and wheel-head, and Celtic carvings on the face. Listed on it are the names of 35 young men from Belhelvie parish. 26 men died in the First World War and nine in the Second World War. They came from all walks of life .

One of the deceased servicemen on the war memorial is Petty Officer George Dallas Forbes D.S.M. who was from Balmedie but left home to seek a life at sea. George was enlisted at The Prince of Wales Sea Training Hostel for Boys, leaving his home in Balmedie. This Merchant Navy seamanship training school was considered to be one of the best and most up-to-date training establishments of its kind in the United Kingdom. The hostel was situated in Church Row, Limehouse, London and contained all the requisite apparatus for nautical instruction which lasted about six months. George subsequently joined the Royal Navy, serving on HMS *Drake*. During the war he served on HMS *Adventure*, a cruiser/mine-layer, HMS *Jupiter*, a destroyer which he had left by the time she struck a mine and sank during the battle of Java Sea. In 1940 George underwent submariner training and joined the submarine HMS *Unbeaten*. In 1942 the *Unbeaten* torpedoed and sank the German submarine *U-374*. George courageously rescued a German submariner Hans Ploch from the sea, the only survivor. Soon after, the *Unbeaten* went missing at sea and George was posthumously awarded the Distinguished Service Medal. After he went missing, his mother never locked her front door until the day she died, hoping for him to return.

The Victoria Hall, with a seating capacity of 400, was built to coincide with Queen Victoria's Diamond Jubilee in 1897. The Hall was the venue for many weddings and local community events such as the annual Salmon Fishers' Ball. Ann Pearson was born in Balmedie in 1910. In 1996 she wrote: *"in 1935 I married Tom Pearson. The wedding was at the Victoria Hall. Mr Ewen was the minister. In those days the minister always kissed the bride! We had a reception for 56 adults and 4 children. The total bill came to £13.6/- which included high tea for all, a bottle of whisky, a bottle of port, a bottle of ginger wine and the wedding cake"*. For a time the hall also housed a library, but this service was taken over by branches of the County Library. In the 1980s an appraisal of the hall concluded it would need £64,000 spent on repairs and modernisation. The trustees unable to raise the funds for its renovation, closed the hall and it lay unused for several years. It has since become a used car dealership. A new manse was built next to the church in 1995 and a church hall, named after Rev, Forsyth was built in 2000, with an extension added in 2021.

Potterton Shop, picture taken in 1960's, in the village of Potterton. The shop (including Post Office) was owned and managed by the same family for 65 years until 2022 when it closed because of retirement. In 1957, Pat and Henry Smith took a leap of faith committing themselves to a mortgage to buy the shop. They later built a garage and filling station opposite the shop. Three generations of the family served the community for all those years with the shop acting as a focal point for local folks. In 1870 Potterton Estate was owned by Reverend John Allan and his wife Margaret who lived at Potterton House. Apart from the mansion house, the estate was comprised of seven farms, two crofts, gardens and a property with the intriguing name of Picktarnity Park (definitions of this word include a black-headed gull, or a thin, wretched-looking person, an ill-cared-for wretch, or a bad-tempered person!) Under separate ownership at the time were two shops with houses and yards attached. From 1843, Potterton had its own Free Church – Belhelvie South, and a school - Wester Hatton, which were built on land gifted by Thomas Clapperton, a druggist. The church is now converted to a residential property, and the school is now Potterton Community Centre.

Lord John Tweedsmuir, who was the son of author John Buchan, moved to Potterton House in 1952 with his wife and daughter, where they are photographed. In 1968 he wrote: *"we live near the city, but we live close to the land in Belhelvie. few of us would exchange it for anywhere else"*. Which kind of sums up the parish of Belhelvie!

photo courtesy of Jane Brownlie Parker

Courtesy of Buchan Heritage Society

There is now just one primary school in Belhelvie parish, in Balmedie village. When the valuation roll was compiled in 1870, there were four schools in the parish which were run by four of the landowners, at Menie, Balmedie, Craigie and Potterton. The Education Act 1872 (Scotland) created school boards in Scotland with a statutory duty to provide education for boys and girls between the ages of 5 and 13. The boards had an elected membership made up of owners and occupiers of property of the value of £4 or over and were responsible for the building and maintenance of schools, staffing and attendance of pupils. They were overseen by the Scotch Board of Education. The Education Act 1901 (Scotland) raised the school leaving age to 14. The Education Act 1918 (Scotland) abolished school boards which were replaced by education authorities and school management committees. In 1870 the schoolhouse at Menie (*above*) was occupied by the Misses Turner who owned Menie Estate. This photograph was taken by James Morrison who took many photographs between 1890 and 1925. The teacher was his sister. Menie School closed in 1949 due to a continuous decrease in enrolment. The remaining students were transferred to Foveran and Balmedie schools.

Mr Troup was a carpenter and wheelwright at Menie. In the 19th century almost every village had a wheelwright who was essential to the movement of goods by cart. Across the road from Mr Troup's workshop was Menie Smithy, home of the blacksmith, conveniently placed as both craftsmen worked closely together, combining their skills.

The Newburgh to Aberdeen Schoolhill bus photographed at Delfrigs, which was part of the Menie Estate, at the northern edge of Belhelvie Parish. Behind the bus are a general shop owned by Alex Cross and Menie Smithy. In 1870, the Delfrigs Croft and Smithy was leased to George Coutts. Sadly the name Coutts appears elsewhere in the parish as George's descendant, Edward Coutts, who served in the Gordon Highlanders is named on the war memorial in Belhelvie Churchyard. He was just 20 years old when he died in July 1916 in the First World War. This bus service was operated by the Great North of Scotland Railway from 1907.

photo Courtesy of Great North of Scotland Railway Association

In the 1870 valuation roll, one of the entries for Menie Estate was a coastguard preventive station, with the house and grounds owned by Lords Commissioners of the Admiralty. This photo shows members of Belhelvie Coastguard Life Saving Apparatus team in 1948 who were awarded a silver shield for the Best Rescue of the Year, rescuing the twelve man crew of the Aberdeen trawler *Northman* which ran aground on the Menie Sands on 5th February 1948. The four men in uniform were paid staff, including the chief coastguard for the area and three officers who lived at Menie Coastguard Cottages at Leyton. The other men were all volunteers from the local community who gave up their time to rescue people in danger along the coastline and in the North Sea.

First Prize Harness.
BELHELVIE,
PLOUGHING MATCH 1908.

Courtesy of Buchan Heritage Society

The Clydesdale is a Scottish breed of draught-horse and is named for its area of origin, the dale or valley of the River Clyde in the west of Scotland. The origins of the breed lie in the 18th century, when Flemish stallions were imported to Scotland to breed with local mares. It is a large and powerful horse, traditionally used for draught power both in farming and in road haulage. In 1877 the Clydesdale Horse Society of Scotland was formed. Large numbers of Clydesdales were exported from Scotland in the late 19th and early 20th century with over 1600 stallions leaving the country in 1911 alone. During the First World War, thousands of horses were conscripted for the war effort and after the war breed numbers declined as farms became increasingly mechanised.

At Easter Hatton a pair of Clydesdale horses dressed for a show with their horseman in his nicky tams around his trousers to keep out dust and vermin, his pocket watch and Albert chain proudly worn. Harness comprises a padded leather collar with iron hames which are curved to the shape of the neck, adjustable with a chain under the neck and a leather belt and buckle at the top of the neck. Sturdy metal hooks low down on the hames attach the traces that transfer the power of the horse to the plough or vehicle. Another set of hooks on the hames at the top of the neck feed the reins from the horseman to the bit in the horse's mouth. The decorated bridle holds the bit in place. Easter Hatton was on the Millden estate owned in the 19th century by Robert Still with several tenants over the years. By 1885, the tenant was Isaac Scott and the owner became Colonel George Leith Fraser towards the end of the century. Isaac Scott bred Clydesdales and showed them at the Kittybrewster Mart in Aberdeen. At this time, Easter Hatton comprised in excess of 340 acres of land, five houses and salmon fishings at the coast. The estate later passed to Major Forbes Leith Fraser and the tenancy to Adam Buchan. When Mr Buchan died, after living at Easter Hatton for 18 years, the 1st Aberdeen Girl Rangers formed a guard of honour at the church in memory of his generosity in allowing them to camp on Easter Hatton each summer. After several changes of owner and occupier, the farm is now home to a waste management company.

Courtesy of Buchan Heritage Society

In 19th century and early 20th century horses especially Clydesdales were essential features of Belhelvie parish farms. William Harry Lumsden of Balmedie House was well known for his love and knowledge of Clydesdale horses and owned Balmedie Clydesdale Stud which he founded in 1883. Just after his death in 1900 *Aberdeen Weekly Journal* reported, *"It is always a matter of deep regret when for any reason a well-known established stud of horses has to be broken up but probably there is no case in the county of Aberdeen in which the scattering of a stud would be regarded with more regretful concern than the dispersion of the Balmedie Clydesdales, so carefully founded by the late W. H. Lumsden and watched by him with ever-deepening interest as his ideals were being realised"*. The Balmedie Clydesdales were well known in horse-breeding circles. In all 18 members of the stud were sold at auction in Perth. The former stables of Balmedie House are now converted into flats and houses. It seems likely that some of the horses were also stabled at Blairton Farm, which at that time was owned by Mr Lumsden.

Courtesy of Buchan Heritage Society

Blairton Farm, Balmedie in 1870 was part of Blairton Estate, owned by a James Walker. The estate also included the Mill of Blairton, the Blairton Inn and shop, a toll-house and salmon fisheries leased from Her Majesty's Woods and Forests. By 1900 the estate had been bought by William Harry Lumsden, owner of Balmedie Estate and breeder of Clydesdale horses. There are five pairs of horses in this picture, It may be that they were all used on the farm, but perhaps they were also coach horses, as Blairton Farm with its stables are roughly halfway between Aberdeen and Newburgh on the main coaching route. The farm house and buildings in these Blairton pictures still stand.

This photo of the Blairton Inn when licensee was James Watt was taken in the early 1900s and still hangs in the pub/restaurant. The Blairton Inn has been a public house for many years, In 1870 it was part of the Blairton Estate, adjoining the Croft of Bridgeton and run by innkeeper David Donald. In 1933, when Blairton and Balmedie Estates were sold after the death of Ernest Lumsden, the Blairton Inn was sold to Castiglioni, who then sold it on to John Baird. He died in 1937, and the pub was run by his widow until 1950. In 1969 the pub was still called the Blairton Inn. By 1979 it had become the Coach and Horses, and then in 1996 was renamed The Cock and Bull.

Blackdog is a small settlement on the north side of Aberdeen City boundary. In the 1870s Blackdog properties were part of the Wester Hatton Estate, owned by the Society of Advocates in Aberdeen who were said to be good landlords. During the time of their ownership of the estate, they built four cottages beside the road to Potterton, appropriately named Advocates' Row. The valuation roll of 1870 lists seven farms, a croft, salmon fishings, shootings and clay-pits within the estate. The Strabathie clay-pits were worked by Seaton Brick and Tile Company who in 1905 leased brickworks, twelve cottages and a special light railway about 3½ miles long which took bricks from Strabathie to the company depot at Bridge of Don. This photo of 1905 shows how clay was dug by squads of four men then transported on a conveyor belt to the works to be made into bricks, tiles and pipes.

At the top of the conveyor belt were the factory buildings of the Seaton Brick and Tile Company, where about 100 people were employed, turning out millions of bricks, thousands of drainpipes and tiles and various other items annually. The photo was taken around 1905. It shows a large kiln with drying loft and chimney on the right, and smaller kiln over to the left. There are three sheds in the centre of the picture where pipes were left to dry after manufacture. Bricks and drainage tiles are stacked in the foreground. The brickworks' own railway engine and carriages waits to transport finished goods to the depot at Bridge of Don. When the brickworks closed in 1924, the railway line was bought by Murcar Golf Club who ran it successfully until 1949.

From the earliest times, the north-east coast of Aberdeenshire was a severe hazard to shipping. Compared to today, early mariners did not have many navigational aids. Lighthouses and beacons were non-existent prior to the 19th century and the rescue of crews was attempted entirely on the initiative of local inhabitants. Lifeboats were progressively stationed round the coast during 19th century, Aberdeen's first was in 1802. The tides along much of the coast are modest in strength, but another hazard was haar or coastal fog. Haar is mainly a summer problem when south-easterly winds cool over the North Sea. These same south-easterly winds blowing for days at a time in winter could produce terrifying storms such as those of January 1800 and November/December 1876, both of which resulted in catastrophic shipping losses around Scotland. Many boats were also lost as a result of wartime activity. Wreckage from the following boats can sometimes be seen at Balmedie Beach, depending on tides and weather conditions. – *The Mary*, wrecked in 1900, *The Star of the Wave* ran aground in 1920, *The Fruitful Bough*, ran aground in 1961 and the *Ross Khartoum* (*above*) which was grounded in 1980.

In the early 1940s a small radar station was installed south of where The Sand Bothy stands today. The remains of three defensive pillboxes can still be seen but there is no obvious trace of the concrete bases for the masts. It is thought that there would have been three masts. Balmedie Beach was also used to destroy enemy ordnance from raids on Aberdeen. In all, Aberdeen was targeted by the Luftwaffe 32 times. On 21st April 1943, Aberdeen was attacked by enemy bombers in what became known as the 'Big Blitz'. A great many lives were lost but thankfully some of the bombs and incendiaries failed to explode. Unexploded bombs were safely detonated on Balmedie Beach far away from buildings. During the Second World War, Dyce was a Fighter Station for 13 Group. Hawker Hurricanes and Supermarine Spitfires were operating out of Dyce as well as aircraft of RAF Coastal Command. To protect this important airfield, a decoy airfield was set up on Harestone Moss, near Whitecairns, complete with runway lights, to divert enemy bombers away from Dyce. Bomb craters still visible on the moss are the only evidence of this area's vital role in the defence of Britain.

Pillboxes are guard posts which were constructed on beaches, at crossroads and on jetties as a defence against invasion. Many were hexagonal and had loopholes on each side to allow firing in all directions. They were easy to defend and provided good protection for the soldiers inside.

Anti-tank blocks were constructed in their thousands in the Second World War to protect vulnerable beaches from attack from the sea. They were generally cubes, either three feet or five feet square. Arranged in rows, they were designed to block the path of a tank or if the tank attempted to drive over the top, the weak underbelly of the tank would be exposed.

Salmon fishers at Eggie (Balmedie) outside their bothy. Sea salmon fishing provided a living for many fishermen for hundreds of years along the north-east coast of Scotland. Within Belhelvie parish there were five salmon fishing stations on the coast, at Menie, Blairton, Eggie (Balmedie), Millden and Blackdog. The fishing season was from February to September. The fishermen used small boats and two different kinds of nets – stake nets which were fixed into the sand on poles, and bag nets, which were moored in deeper water with casks or anchors. Fishing was carried out at high tide. During the season, the fishermen lived in bothies, which were equipped with bunk beds and cooking facilities. Out of season, many fishermen worked on local farms. Salmon fishing finished at Balmedie in the 1990s. An ice house, which was part of Balmedie Estate salmon fishings, can still be found in the sand dunes towards the south of Balmedie Country Park. Fish would be caught and then stored in ice houses until they could be taken to the Fish Market in Aberdeen for sale. Ruins of three of these have been found along this coast with the one near Balmedie Beach the most intact.